THE SOUL OF AMERICA

DR. DAVID JEREMIAH

MULTNOMAH BOOKS • SISTERS, OREGON

THE SOUL OF AMERICA
published by Multnomah Books
a part of the Questar publishing family
©1996 by David Jeremiah

International Standard Book Number: 1-157673-091-3

Cover design by Kevin Keller
Printed in the United States of America

Scripture quotations are from:
The Believer's Study Bible, New King James Version,
©1991 by the Criswell Center for Biblical Studies

For information:
Questar Publishers, Inc. □ Post Office Box 1720 □ Sisters, Oregon 97759

01 02 03 — 10 9 8 7 6 5 4 3 2 1

The Soul of America

HER FOUNDATION

But seek first the kingdom of God and His righteousness,
and all these things shall be added to you.

Matthew 6:33

Although America has only 6 percent of the world's population, more than 50 percent of the modern luxuries that characterize civilization are found in this land.

He teaches my hands to make war,
so that my arms can bend a bow of bronze.
Blessed be the LORD my Rock,
who trains my hands for war, and my fingers for battle.

Psalm 18:34 and 144:1

A GI helicopter pilot was killed, and on his tombstone in New Hampshire his parents had these nineteenth century words inscribed:

"War is an ugly thing, but not the ugliest of things. The decayed and degraded state of moral and patriotic feeling, which thinks nothing is worth a war, is worse. A man who has nothing which he cares more about than his own personal safety is a miserable creature, and has no chance of being free unless he is made free and kept so by the exertions of better men than himself."

John Stuart Mill

And if it seems evil to you to serve the LORD,
choose for yourselves this day whom you will serve,
whether the gods which your fathers served
that were on the other side of the River,
or the gods of the Amorites, in whose land you dwell.
But as for me and my house, we will serve the LORD.

Joshua 24:15

That land is great which knows the Lord,
Whose songs are guided by His Word;
Where justice rules twixt man and man,
Where love controls an ardent plan;
Where, breathing in his native air,
Each soul finds joy in praise and prayer. . .
Thus may our country, good and great,
Be God's delight . . . man's best estate.

author unknown

Both riches and honor come from You, and You reign over all.
In Your hand is power and might;
in Your hand it is to make great and to give strength to all.
Now, therefore, our God, we thank You and praise Your glorious name.

I Chronicles 29:12-13

I have lived, sir, a long time, and the longer I live, the more convincing proof I see of this truth—that God governs in the affairs of men. And if a sparrow cannot fall to the ground without His notice, is it probable that an empire can rise without His aid?

Benjamin Franklin

Open the gates,
that the righteous nation which keeps the truth may enter in.

Isaiah 26:2

Praise the power that hath made and preserved us a nation!
Then conquer we must, when our cause it is just;
And this be our motto: 'In God is our trust'
And the star-spangled banner in triumph shall wave
O'er the land of the free, and the home of the brave.

from our National Anthem

. . .When the LORD your God brings you
into the land of which He swore to your fathers, . . .
to give you large and beautiful cities which you did not build,
houses full of all good things, which you did not fill,
hewn-out wells which you did not dig,
vineyards and olive trees which you did not plant
—when you have eaten and are full—
then beware, lest you forget the LORD. . . .

Deuteronomy 6:10-12

I sought for the greatness and genius of America in her commodious harbors and ample rivers, and it was not there. Not until I went into the churches of America and heard her pulpits aflame with righteousness did I understand the secret of her genius and power. . . . America is great because she is good, and if America ever ceases to be good, we will cease to be great.

Alexis de Tocqueville

The fear of the LORD is the beginning of wisdom,
and the knowledge of the Holy One is understanding.

Proverbs 9:10

In *The Light and the Glory*, Peter Marshall tells of God's superintending hand upon the life of Christopher Columbus. This adventurer discovered the "New World" by accident, but *not* by accident. God had His hand upon the wheel of the ship and brought it here, even though Columbus himself did not know what was happening. George Washington summarized this thought when he said, "No people can be bound to acknowledge and adore the invisible hand which conducts the affairs of man more than those of the United States."

And do not present your members as instruments of unrighteousness to sin,
but present yourselves to God as being alive from the dead,
and your members as instruments of righteousness to God.

Romans 6:13

Men are qualified for civil liberty in exact proportion to their disposition to moral chains upon their own appetites. . . . Society cannot exist unless a controlling power upon will and appetite be placed somewhere; and the less of it there is within, the more there must be without. It is ordained in the eternal constitution of things that men of intemperate minds cannot be free.

Edmund Burke

Be still, and know that I am God;
I will be exalted among the nations,
I will be exalted in the earth!

Psalm 46:10

Dear Father, whom we cannot see,
We know that Thou art near;
With longing hearts we turn to Thee,
And ask that Thou wilt set us free
From war and hate and fear.

John Oxenham

I have not strayed from Your precepts.
Your testimonies I have taken as a heritage forever,
for they are the rejoicing of my heart.
I have inclined my heart to perform Your statutes forever,
to the very end.

Psalm 119:110b-112

In God we trust, let others trust their rulers;
We trust in God to save us from alarm;
Like broken reeds, the works of man will fail us,
Our God alone can keep us from all harm.

Oswald J. Smith

HER FAITH

Blessed is the nation whose God is the LORD,
the people He *has chosen as* His *own inheritance.*

Psalm 33:12

Democracy is another leaf from the book of Christianity, which has also, I fear, been torn out, and while, perhaps not misread, has certainly been half-emptied of meaning by being divorced from its Christian context and secularized.

Arnold Toynbee

And we know that the Son of God has come
and has given us an understanding,
that we may know Him who is true; and we are in Him who is true,
in His Son Jesus Christ.
This is the true God and eternal life.

I John 5:20

Many Americans have high ideals but no transcendent principles upon which to base those ideals. So when you ask them, "Why are you faithful to your spouse?" or "Why do you care about your kids?" they say simply, "It feels right." Not because it is right or wrong, just "it feels right *for me*."

Robert Bellah

"Behold, the days are coming," says the Lord God,
"That I will send a famine on the land,
not a famine of bread, nor a thirst for water,
but of hearing the words of the LORD.
They shall wander from sea to sea, and from north to east;
they shall run to and fro, seeking the word of the LORD,
but shall not find it."

Amos 8:11-12

There is a famine of great preaching, a famine of strong expository preaching, a famine of conscience-stirring preaching, a famine of heartbreaking preaching, a famine of soul-tearing preaching, a famine of that preaching like our fathers knew which kept men awake all night lest they fall into hell. I repeat, "There is a famine of the Word of the Lord."

Leonard Ravenhill

Not forsaking the assembling of ourselves together, as is the manner of some,
but exhorting one another,
and so much the more as you see the Day approaching.

Hebrews 10:25

Several years ago, a survey revealed that when Mom and Dad took (not sent) their children to church, 76 percent of the children followed their parents in their faith. If only the father took the children to church, the percentage dropped to 55 percent. Interestingly enough, if only the mother took the children to church, the percentage dropped to 15 percent. If neither parent took the children to church, only 9 percent became active Christians.

Zig Ziglar

Render therefore to Caesar the things that are Caesar's,
and to God the things that are God's.

Matthew 22:21

History has demonstrated the damage that is done when Caesar attempts to control the church or when the church tries to control Caesar. As Christians, we have a responsibility both to the state and to God. We dare not ignore either. The Christian's highest goal is a free church in a free state. It was Daniel Webster who said, "Whatever makes men good Christians, makes them good citizens."

Render therefore to all their due:
taxes to whom taxes are due,
customs to whom customs,
fear to whom fear,
honor to whom honor.

Romans 13:7

representative of the Roman Empire visiting the province of Palestine shortly after the death and resurrection of Christ reported to the emperor that those calling themselves Christians were characterized by two things, namely, "They sing songs and pay their taxes."

Righteousness exalts a nation,
but sin is a reproach to any people.

Proverbs 14:34

If continental expanse made a nation great, Siberia would be the mightiest country. If concentrated population made a nation great, India would be the greatest nation. If ancient culture made a nation great, China would be the leader of all the families on earth. What makes a nation great? It is the character of the people. A nation is made not by its fruitful acres, but by the men who till them; not by its rich mines, but by the men who work them.

For the word of God is living and powerful,
and sharper than any two-edged sword,
piercing even to the division of soul and spirit,
and of joints and marrow,
and is a discerner of the thoughts and intents of the heart.

Hebrews 4:12

America has been blessed by God because America has honored God and His Word. George Washington ennobled the office of the presidency when he said, "It is impossible to rightly govern the world without God and the Bible." Abraham Lincoln agreed: "I believe the Bible is the best gift God has ever given to man. All the good from the Savior of the world is communicated from this Book."

HER FRIENDS

Now the LORD had said to Abram:

"Get out of your country, from your family and from your father's house,

to a land that I will show you.

I will make you a great nation;

I will bless you and make your name great;

and you shall be a blessing.

I will bless those who bless you,

and I will curse him who curses you;

and in you all the families of the earth shall be blessed.

Genesis 12:1-3

Frederick the Great of Germany was something of a skeptic because of his association with Voltaire, the French infidel. On one occasion he addressed his court chaplain with these words: "Give me proof that the Bible is a Divine Book."

His chaplain replied, "The Jew, your Majesty, the Jew."

For you are a holy people to the LORD your God;
the LORD your God has chosen you to be a people for Himself,
a special treasure above all the peoples of the earth.
The LORD did not set His love on you nor choose you because you were more in
number than any other people,
for you were the least of all peoples.

Deuteronomy 7:6-7

Jews constitute one percent of the human race. It suggests a nebulous, dim puff of star dust in the blaze of the Milky Way. Properly the Jew ought hardly to be heard of, but he is heard of. He is as prominent on this planet as any other people. His commercial importance is extravagantly out of proportion to the smallness of his bulk. His contributions to the world's list of great names in literature, science, art, music, finance, medicine and abstruse learning are also altogether out of proportion to the weakness of his numbers. He has made a marvelous fight in the world in all ages and he has done it with his hands tied behind him.

Walter B. Knight

Thus says the LORD, Who gives the sun for a light by day,
the ordinances of the moon and the stars for a light by night,
who disturbs the sea, and its waves roar (The LORD of Hosts is His name):
"If those ordinances depart from before Me," says the LORD,
"then the seed of Israel shall also cease from being a nation before Me forever."
Thus says the LORD: "If heaven above can be measured,
and the foundations of the earth searched out beneath,
I will also cast off all the seed of Israel for all that they have done,"
says the LORD.

Jeremiah 31:35-37

It is as impossible to get rid of the Jew as it is to pull the sun from its orbit. It is as impossible to move the Jew out of his place as it is to move the planets out of their spheres. It is as impossible to prevent the Jew from coming to the ultimate end and place that God has for him as it is to shake the heavens and move them out of their ultimate habitation.

For thus says the LORD of hosts:
"He sent Me after glory, to the nations which plunder you;
for he who touches you touches the apple of His eye."

Zechariah 2:8

Remarkable and abundant provision is made for the protection of the eye. The protection consists of (1) the strong frontal bones to guard against a blow, (2) the brow and eyelash to protect against dust, (3) the lid to guard against glare, and (4) the tear gland to provide continuous cleansing. With Israel is the omnipotent power of God committed to protect them.

Charles Feinberg

I will open my mouth in a parable;
I will utter dark sayings of old, which we have heard and known,
and our fathers have told us.
We will not hide them from their children,
telling to the generation to come the praise of the LORD,
and His strength and His wonderful works that He has done.

Psalm 78:2-4

I have on my desk an old, old photograph. It is a photograph of my great grandfather who was a farmer in Aberdineshire, Scotland. The photograph is almost faded out with age, though I have tried to keep it covered from the light, because I wanted to have it as long as I might live. People who knew my grandfather told me that he used to gather all his large family and his many farmhands together at the end of each day and pray for the salvation and blessing of his children and his children's children unto the third and fourth generation. As I look at the grizzled face of that old Scottish farmer, I thank God for his prayers and for the way He answered them in my life.

Harry Ironside

For I am not ashamed of the gospel of Christ, for it is the power of God to salvation for everyone who believes, for the Jew first and also for the Greek.

Romans 1:16

We are told the famous British actor Garrick was once asked by a bishop how it was that he produced far more powerful results by fiction than the bishops could by preaching the truth. The reply of the actor is full of force. "My Lord," he said, "the reason is obvious. I speak fiction as though it were truth, whereas you speak truth as though it were fiction."

Do not be unequally yoked together with unbelievers.
For what fellowship has righteousness with lawlessness?
And what communion has light with darkness?

II Corinthians 6:14

Man is essentially a religious being. Because of this, some of the strongest feelings of life are our spiritual convictions. We die for them. It is difficult to see how two people of diverse religious viewpoints can get along well for any length of time if they are well grounded in their different beliefs. It may work well for a season; but when sickness, sorrow, infirmities, or adversities come, each will likely run back to his faith for help, and the rift between the two will widen.

Dr. Joseph M. Stowell

Her Families

Unless the LORD builds the house,
they labor in vain who build it;
unless the LORD guards the city,
the watchman stays awake in vain.

Psalm 127:1

So long as we have homes where lamps are lit
and prayers are said,

Although a people falter through the dark
and nations grope,

With God, Himself, back of these little homes
we still have hope.

Grace Noll Crowell

But if anyone does not provide for his own,
and especially for those of his household,
he has denied the faith and is worse than an unbeliever.

I Timothy 5:8

In reading this passage we might believe that Paul's primary focus is on the provision of food, shelter, and clothing. But I believe God holds the Christian father equally responsible for those needs which can only be met by his ongoing personal involvement with his family.

Husbands, likewise, dwell with them with understanding,
giving honor to the wife, as to the weaker vessel,
and as being heirs together of the grace of life,
that your prayers may not be hindered.

I Peter 3:7

I love you
Not only for what you are,
But for what I am
When I am with you.
I love you
Not only for what
You have made of yourself,
But for what
You are making of me.

Mary Carolyn Davis

Train up a child in the way he should go,
and when he is old he will not depart from it.

Proverbs 22:6

What about Proverbs 22:6? If you examine its context, you will discover that the verse is not a promise made by God to anybody. It is a statement, a general statement about how family relationships normally work . . . It tells us what we can see around us if we only open our eyes. Good parents usually produce good children . . . but when we interpret it as inflexible law, we are reading into it something the Holy Spirit never intended.

John White

These things command and teach.
Let no one despise your youth,
but be an example to the believers
in word, in conduct, in love, in spirit, in faith, in purity.

I Timothy 4:11-12

Today there are Bible stories to read, cassettes to hear, and games to play. Never before has there been such an abundance of Christian music and concerts. Learn some of the catchy songs that children enjoy; sing them when you're in the car or around the house. Too many kids seem to know more jingles from television commercials than they do songs about Jesus.

And these words which I command you today shall be in your heart.
You shall teach them diligently to your children,
and shall talk of them when you sit in your house,
when you walk by the way, when you lie down, and when you rise up.
You shall bind them as a sign on your hand,
and they shall be as frontlets between your eyes.
You shall write them on the doorposts of your house and on your gates.

Deuteronomy 6:6-9

I saw you stand bravely through the years
And saw no sign of senseless fears
I saw you stand quietly through the stress
And saw no glimpse of bitterness
I saw you stand prayerfully in grief
And saw no sign of unbelief
Though you spoke well of Jesus Christ
I caught your faith by watching your life.

author unknown

He who spares his rod hates his son,
but he who loves him disciplines him promptly.

Proverbs 13:24

The parent has got to convince himself that discipline is not something that he does to the child, but something he does for the child. His attitude toward the child must be, "I love you too much to let you behave like that."

Dr. James Dobson

But if you are without chastening,
of which all have become partakers,
then you are illegitimate and not sons.

Hebrews 12:8

Unfortunately, there are many sons (and daughters) who have never been corrected. Either through misguided love or neglect, they have been allowed to grow up free as unguided missiles. It is love, not anger, nor frustration, nor impatience that should be the motive to move a parent to discipline.

And you, fathers, do not provoke your children to wrath,
but bring them up in the training and admonition of the Lord.

Ephesians 6:4

The King James version says, "Provoke not your children to wrath." We provoke when we're on their case all the time. The easiest way to separate us from our children is to use sarcasm or snide remarks about their appearance or behavior, particularly in front of others. We exasperate our children by imposing punishment for one child and ignoring bad behavior in another.

Do not be deceived, God is not mocked;

for whatever a man sows, that he will also reap.

For he who sows to his flesh will of the flesh reap corruption,

but he who sows to the Spirit will of the Spirit reap everlasting life.

Galatians 6:7-8

We are drowning our young people in violence, cynicism, and sadism. Someone has observed that the grandchildren of the kids who used to weep because the little match girl froze to death now feel cheated if she is not slugged, raped, and thrown into a furnace.

[The Elijah who is to come] will turn the hearts of the fathers to the children,
and the hearts of the children to their fathers,
lest I come and strike the earth with a curse.

Malachi 4:6

C learly the Old Testament, from beginning to end, upholds the importance of the family. Though the information covers a time period of two thousand years, there is no indication that God changed His mind about the original blueprint given in Genesis 1-3. The family is just as important in Malachi's day as it is in the Garden of Eden.

But you must continue
in the things which you have learned and been assured of,
knowing from whom you have learned them,
and that from childhood you have known the Holy Scriptures,
which are able to make you wise for salvation
through faith which is in Christ Jesus.

II Timothy 3:14-15

God planned the family. He made it the keystone in human living. It launches human beings into the world; it starts them out on their journey of life; it protects them in mind and body in their first perilous years and helps to develop in them the personality which they will have for life. Above all, the family is God's instrument to insert into people the life which they do not have by physical birth, the life which God Himself must give through His Spirit and because of Jesus Christ.

Oscar Feucht

HER FAILURES

For My people have committed two evils:
they have forsaken Me, the fountain of living waters,
and hewn themselves cisterns—broken cisterns that can hold no water.

Jeremiah 2:13

Where is the God of our fathers;
the God of America's birth?
The God that we once believed sovereign,
and maker of heaven and earth?
We now have found us some new gods,
which we worship and serve as a slave;
For the God of the Bible's forgotten
in the land of the free and the brave.

author unknown

The priests did not say, "Where is the LORD?"
and those who handle the law did not know Me;
the rulers also transgressed against me;
the prophets prophesied by Baal,
and walked after things that do not profit.

Jeremiah 2:8

Spiritual adultery is worse . . . than physical adultery. But it is also much worse . . . than the Jews following their idols. Oh, how God spoke out against the Jews following their idols.... But modern liberal theology is far worse than this. For, it turns against greater light, against greater blessing.

Francis Schaeffer

Hell and Destruction are never full;
so the eyes of man are never satisfied.

Proverbs 27:20

A man who sets out on a journey of self-indulgence will ultimately die at the hand of his own lust.

I have made a covenant with my eyes;
why then should I look upon a young woman?

Job 31:1

Keeping ourselves pure before God will not come easily to modern Christians. Without a plan to deal with this area of life, all of us are subject to defeat. Perhaps the following suggestions will help those who struggle in this matter.

A good man out of the good treasure of his heart brings forth good; and an evil man out of the evil treasure of his heart brings forth evil. For out of the abundance of the heart his mouth speaks.

Luke 6:45

The mind is the battleground upon which every moral and spiritual battle is fought. As far back as Noah, this has been true. When God saw the "great wickedness" of Noah's day, He perceived that every intent of the thoughts of man's heart "was only evil continually" (Genesis 6:5).

For we are not ignorant of [Satan's] devices.

II Corinthians 2:11

I am convinced that as Satan goes about seeking whom he may devour, he has a definite strategy for each of us. I am quite often surprised by the consistency of sinning Christians. Same time, same place, same companions, same circumstances, over and over again. Satan knows our weaknesses and uses all the tools at his command to keep us constantly in great spiritual jeopardy.

How can a young man cleanse his way?
By taking heed according to Your word.
Your word I have hidden in my heart,
that I might not sin against You.

Psalm 119:9, 11

When we have committed many passages of God's Word to memory, we will discover that they come to our minds at just the right moment to aid us in gaining victory in this battle.

In those days there was no king in Israel;
everyone did what was right in his own eyes.

Judges 21:25

Notice that the Bible does not say they did wrong, but rather that every man did what was right as he saw it. Man became his own god, which was nothing less than secular humanism in its purest form.

For You formed my inward parts; You covered me in my mother's womb.
I will praise You, for I am fearfully and wonderfully made;
marvelous are Your works, and that my soul knows very well.
My frame was not hidden from You, when I was made in secret, and skillfully
wrought in the lowest parts of the earth.
Your eyes saw my substance, being yet unformed.
And in Your book they all were written,
the days fashioned for me, when as yet there were none of them.

Psalm 139:13-16

I will never walk the shores of life
Or know the tides of time;
For I was coming but unloved
And that my only crime.

author unknown

But Jesus said,
"Let the little children come to Me,
and do not forbid them;
for of such is the kingdom of heaven."

Matthew 19:14

The intention of God for every child conceived in the womb is that he grow up into God's kingdom, that he pass one day through the portals of death into life everlasting with God Himself. This is why Jesus said, "See that you do not despise one of these little ones."

Your hands have made me and fashioned me, an intricate unity;
yet You would destroy me.
Remember, I pray, that You have made me like clay.
And will You turn me into dust again?
Did You not pour me out like milk, and curdle me like cheese,
clothe me with skin and flesh, and knit me together with bones and sinews?
You have granted me life and favor,
and Your care has preserved my spirit.

Job 10:8-12

The abortionists seem to forget easily, or perhaps refuse altogether to consider, that from the very moment of conception, the hopes and dreams and plans of an almighty God are set in motion for each individual.

Pride goes before destruction,
and a haughty spirit before a fall.

Proverbs 16:18

Pride is the essential vice, the utmost evil.... Unchastity, anger, greed, drunkenness, and all that, are mere flea bites in comparison. It was through pride that the devil became the Devil. Pride leads to every other vice. It is the complete anti-God state of mind. A proud man is always looking down on things and people: and, of course, as long as you are looking down, you cannot see something that is above you.

C. S. Lewis

And such were some of you.
But you were washed, but you were sanctified, but you were justified
in the name of the Lord Jesus and by the Spirit of our God.
I Corinthians 6:11

This is a faithful saying and worthy of all acceptance,
that Christ Jesus came into the world to save sinners,
of whom I am chief.
I Timothy 1:15

It is interesting to note that in the context of two passages in which Paul addressed the subject of homosexuality, he held out the only hope of recovery for the homosexual as being in the person of the Lord Jesus Christ.

Have you not read that He who made them at the beginning
made them male and female,
and said, "For this reason a man shall leave his father and mother
and be joined to his wife, and the two shall become one flesh"?
So then, they are no longer two but one flesh.
Therefore what God has joined together, let not man separate.

Matthew 19:4-6

Sometimes it is argued that Jesus never mentioned homosexuality in the Gospels, therefore it must be all right. The age-old argument that silence means consent can be mighty handy when one is on the wrong side of the truth. The fact is, however, that when Jesus spoke about human sexuality, He always presupposed heterosexuality.

For this reason God gave them up to vile passions.
For even their women exchanged the natural use for what is against nature.
Likewise also the men, leaving the natural use of the woman,
burned in their lust for one another.

Romans 1:26-27a

Paul teaches that the wrath of God is revealed from heaven against those who turn from their proper relationship to the Creator, holding down the truth of God, and practicing idolatry. Men who give up God are given up by God to wander in moral pollution.

According to Paul, homosexuality is the cultural culmination of rebellion against God. It is symptomatic of a society under judgment, inwardly corrupted to the point of collapse.

Do not be deceived.
Neither fornicators, nor idolaters, nor adulterers, nor homosexuals . . .
will inherit the kingdom of God.

I Corinthians 6:9-10

Here Paul uses two Greek words to refer to homosexuality: *malakio* and *arsenokoitai*. These two words were used consistently by Greek authors to apply to the full spectrum of homosexuality. Only the wildest of religious speculations can avoid the conclusion that Paul knew both exactly what he meant and how he would be understood when he used those terms.

For the hearts of this people have grown dull.
Their ears are hard of hearing, and their eyes they have closed,
lest they should see with their eyes and hear with their ears,
lest they should understand with their hearts
and turn, so that I should heal them.

Acts 28:27

Let us remember that all the mischief, all the corruption and confusion, all the shame and dishonor, all the reproach and blasphemy, had its origin in the neglect of the Word of God. . . . It has ever been the special design of Satan to lead God's people away from Scripture. He will use anything and everything for this end — tradition — the church, so-called — expediency — human reason — popular opinion — reputation and influence — character, position, and usefulness — all those he will use in order to get the heart and conscience away from that one golden sentence—that divine motto, "It is written."

C. H. MacKintosh

HER FUTURE?

If My people who are called by My name
will humble themselves,
and pray and seek My face,
and turn from their wicked ways,
then I will hear from heaven,
and will forgive their sin and heal their land.

II Chronicles 7:14

In the middle of the nineteenth century, when our nation was divided over the issue of slavery, and people were living in a selfish, materialistic approach to life, God raised up Jeremiah Lamphier to lead a revival of prayer. In 1857, he began a prayer meeting in the upper room of the Old Fulton Street Dutch Reformed Church in Manhattan. Beginning with only six people, the prayer meeting grew until the church was filled with praying people. By February of 1858, nearly ten thousand people a week were being converted. The impact of these prayer meetings spread from city to city across the United States. Cleveland, Detroit, Chicago, Cincinnati—city after city was conquered by the power of believing prayer.

Beware that you do not forget the LORD your God . . .
lest—when you have eaten and are full, . . .
and your silver and your gold are multiplied, . . .
when your heart is lifted up, and you forget the LORD your God. . .
[and] say in your heart,
"My power and the might of my hand have gained me this wealth." . . .
If you by any means forget the LORD your God . . .
I testify against you this day that you shall surely perish.

Deuteronomy 8:11-14, 17, 19

A democracy cannot exist as a permanent form of government. It can only exist until the voters discover that they can vote themselves money from the public treasury. From that moment on, the majority always votes for the candidates promising the most money from the public treasury, with the result that a democracy always collapses over loose fiscal policy, always followed by dictatorship.

Alexander Tyler

Their inward part is destruction. . . .
Pronounce them guilty, O God!
Let them fall by their own counsels.

Psalm 5:9-10

One of the great masterpieces of all time is Edward Gibbon's *The Decline and Fall of the Roman Empire*. The thesis of that survey of ancient Rome is this, "That it fell, not because of the superior enemy on the outside but because of the decay of Rome on the inside." Rome was not murdered, she committed suicide.

So I sought for a man among them who would make a wall,
and stand in the gap before Me on behalf of the land,
that I should not destroy it;
but I found no one.

Ezekiel 22:30

In Germany they came first for the Communist, and I didn't speak up because I wasn't a Communist. Then they came for the Jews, and I didn't speak up because I wasn't a Jew. Then they came for the trade unionists, and I didn't speak up because I wasn't a trade unionist. Then they came for the Catholics, and I didn't speak up because I was a Protestant. Then they came for me, and by that time, no one was left to speak up.

Martin Niemoller

The LORD . . . looked for justice, but behold, oppression;
for righteousness, but behold,
a cry for help.

Isaiah 5:7

The average age of the world's great civilizations has been 200 years. These nations have progressed through the following sequence: From bondage to spiritual faith, from spiritual faith to great courage, from courage to liberty, from liberty to abundance, from abundance to selfishness, from selfishness to complacency, from complacency to apathy, from apathy to dependency, and from dependency back to bondage.

Alexander Tyler

The wicked shall be turned into hell,
and all the nations that forget God.

Psalm 9:17

Your republic will be fearfully plundered and laid waste by barbarians in the twentieth century, with this difference: The Huns and the Vandals who ransacked Rome were from without, and your Huns and Vandals will come from within your own country, and be engendered from within by your own institutions.

Thomas Macaulay

Because the sentence against an evil work
is not executed speedily, therefore
the heart of the sons of men is fully set in them to do evil

Ecclesiastes 8:11

Though the mills of God grind slowly
    Yet they grind exceeding small.
Though with patience He stands waiting
    With exactness grinds He all.

*Of the increase of His government
and peace
there will be no end. . . .*

Isaiah 9:7

The Prince of Peace is coming,
 Earth's rightful Lord and King,
 He'll still the warring nations,
And truth and justice bring,
No other one can do it.
And cause the longed-for peace;
He, He alone is able,
"He maketh wars to cease."

author unknown

About the Author

DR. DAVID JEREMIAH is the founder of Turning Point, a ministry committed to providing Christians with sound Bible teaching relevant to today's changing times through radio broadcasts, audiocassette series, study guides and books. Dr. Jeremiah's "common sense" Biblical exposition and teaching on such topics as family, stress, the New Age, and Biblical prophecy forms the foundation of Turning Point Ministries.

Dr. Jeremiah is the Senior Pastor of Shadow Mountain Community Church in El Cajon, San Diego County, California, where he also serves as President of Christian Heritage College. He and his wife Donna have four children.

In 1982 Dr. Jeremiah began bringing the same solid teaching to San Diego television that he shared weekly with his congregation via a new ministry called Turning Point. Shortly thereafter, the work was expanded to radio, and currently Dr. Jeremiah's inspiring messages are broadcast daily on over 350 national and international radio stations.

Because Dr. Jeremiah desires to know his listening audience, he travels nationwide holding radio rallies and enrichment conferences which touch the hearts and lives of many. According to Dr. Jeremiah, "At some point in time, everyone reaches a Turning Point, and, for every person, that moment is unique, an experience to hold onto forever. There's so much changing in today's world, sometimes it's difficult to choose the right path. Turning Point offers people an understanding of God's Word, as well as the opportunity to make a difference in the world."